"My faith, my strength"

FIVE MYSTERIES OF FAITH

THE FIVE

MYSTERIES

OF

FAITH.

My Faith, My Strength

"My faith, my strength"

THE FIVE

MYSTERIES

OF

FAITH.

My Faith, My Strength

WRITTEN BY

MAGNUS I. NNAJI

©2023 Magnus I Nnaji. All rights reserved. Unauthorized reproduction or use of this book or its contents, including photocopying, filming, or electronic transmission, without the express written permission of the publisher, is strictly prohibited.

DEDICATION

To all seekers of truth and wisdom,

May this book be a beacon of light on your journey of faith.

To my loved ones, who have supported me with unwavering love and encouragement,

Thank you for being my rock and my inspiration.

To the countless individuals who have shaped my understanding of faith,

Your insights and perspectives have enriched my life and this book.

May we all continue to seek, to question, and to deepen our understanding of the mysteries of faith.

With love and gratitude,

Magnus I NNAJI

ACKNOWLEDGMENT

I express my gratitude to:

- The Almighty for the gift of curiosity and passion for truth
- Family, friends, and mentors for their love and support
- Scholars and writers whose works have influenced my thoughts
- Publishers and editors for their expertise and dedication
- Readers who have accompanied me on this journey of exploration

May this book be a blessing to all who read it.

"My faith, my strength"

Table Of Contents

- ☐ Dedication.------------------------ 4
- ☐ Acknowledgement.------------ 5
- ☐ Table of Contents.-------------- 6

☐ Introduction ---------------- 8
1. The meaning of Mystery ------------------ 8
2. The meaning of Faith ---------------------- 9
3. The Five(5) mysteries of Faith ----------- 10

☐ Chapter One----------------12
1. First mystery (Miracle of Reconciliation 13
2. Know Your Faith ----------------------------- 14
3. Story of ignorant Airplane Cleaner ------ 16
4. Things to know about Faith ---------------- 18
5. The 15 Article of Believe -------------------- 20
6. Maria Faustina prayer in time of suffering 23
7. Three (3) Goals to achieve in Faith ----- 26

☐ Chapter Two. ------------------------- 30
1. Believe in your Faith. ----------------------- 31

2. 2nd Mystery (miracle of wealth) ---------- 31
3. How to develop a stubborn Faith --------- 37
4. Story of a Thomas Fish --------------------- 43

Chapter Three. ——————— 47
1. Irreparable hope and Trust ----------------- 48
2. 3rd Mystery (miracle of calming the storm) 48
3. Definition of Hope ------------------------- 50
4. Hope Theory ------------------------------- 52
5. Irreparable hope in Faith irresistible ----- 53
6. Irreparable Hope as a Therapy ------------ 54
7. Great men's Quotes on irreparable Trust 62

Chapter Four. ——————— 65
1. Take a positive action --------------------- 66
2. 4th Mystery (Miracle of Healing ---------- 66
3. Fourteen Humanitarian Actions ---------- 71
4. How a Smithman refines a silver --------- 74

Chapter FIVE. ——————— 76
1) 5Th Mystery (Hold on persistence) ------ 77
2) The parables of the persistent widow --- 77
3) Persistence --------------------------------- 78
4) The important of persistent in prayer ---- 79
5) My persistent story ------------------------ 80
6) Relationship between failure and persistence 81
7) Story Examples of Fail and persisted Heroes 81
8) Benefits of persistence ------------------- 86
9) Some Biblical quotes for persistence ---- 88

INTRODUCTIONS

The MEANING OF MYSTERY

Mystery simple mean, anything that is kept secret or remains unexplained or unknown: the mysteries of nature. any affair, thing, or person that presents features or qualities so obscure as to arouse curiosity or speculation: The masked guest is an absolute mystery to everyone.
A "mystery" in the New Testament is something that had at one time been hidden but is now revealed to God's people. Jesus spoke of "the mystery of the kingdom of God " (Mark 4:11,) that He was at that point revealing to His disciples.

Paul said that he had been commissioned to preach "the word of God in its fullness the mystery that has been kept hidden for ages and generations, but is now disclosed to the Lord's people " (Colossians 1:25–26). represent the final disclosure of God's Word to mankind.

THE MEANING OF the FAITH

In the context of religion, one can define faith as confidence or trust in a particular system of religious belief, which faith may equate to confidence based on some perceived degree of warrant, in contrast to a definition of faith as being belief without evidence.
Faith is a gift of the holy spirit which helps somebody to believe without thinking negatively on whatever God reveals.

According to an advanced learners dictionary, faith is defined as trust and complete confidence .Also faith is being loyal to somebody over a long period of time
.
Perhaps , faith may be characterized by trust , loyalty, belief , and nonfiction. Let's recap, I don't want to say much on faith itself, since many people have written on it. Let's focus on its five mysteries.

The Five mysteries in faith

Words or phrases that are only used one time and that do not have a clear definition in that passage can be difficult to interpret. Therefore, I admit that my understanding of the five mysteries of the faith is not as secure as with many doctrines. However, I do think that we can get a pretty good understanding of what is being referred to here.

The word "mystery" is commonly used in Paul's epistles. In a previous study, I have seen four references of mysteries in the Bible. They are:
Understanding of previous mysteries (Ephesians 3:4-5-9, Matthew 13:35) but we speak God's word secret and hidden (1 Corinthians 2:7-10) to you you have been given the secret of the kingdom of God. (Matthew 13:10-11; Ephesians 3:10) Meant to be taught (1 Corinthians 4:1-2)

Therefore, we are looking for something that has not been revealed to Old Testament saints but is an important part of New Testament understanding.

I notice the phrasing of the mystery. It is not the five mystery of faith, but "The five mystery in faith." The first occurred in the Bible in (John 3;1:21) as Nicodemus secretly went to Jesus in the night to know the faith of the kingdom of God.
As in (John 3:16),
Acts 3:16 And his name through faith in his name hath made this man strong, whom ye see and know: yea, THE FAITH which is by him hath given him this perfect soundness in the presence of you all.

The five mysteries in faith are (FAITH) it self is what practicable, one need attention on this mysteries for it helps in all rounds of life.

The five mysteries in faith

- **F**   **First known the articles**
- **A**   **Arise and believe in those articles**
- **I**   **Irresistible trust and hope in your believe**
- **T**   **Take positive Actions and prove your faith**
- **H**   **Hold on persistence.**

"My faith, my strength"

CHAPTER ONE

FIRST KNOW THE ARTICLES

"My faith, my strength"

FIRST KNOWN YOUR FAITH

1ST MYSTERY

Miracle of reconciliation

Searching for the knowledge of faith.

Nicodemus secretly moving to Jesus to known the secret of that he is about to believe as a faith (john:3v1-25)

Many Rich men, unlike Nicodemus, didn't have this grace, just like in the episode of (Jesus and the young Rich ruler, Mark 10;17:31).

When Jesus came to the place, he looked up, and saw him, and said unto him, Zacchaeus, make haste, and come down; for today I must abide at thy house (Luke :19v5) few chose to sick his face and knowledge.

This when God chooses to reconcile with merely man so that he can come close and know the secret of heaven and of his faith . "#know your faith"

KNOW YOUR FAITH

Known what you tend to have or already has as faith
One needs to study seriously his article of faith before believing it. This is very paramount important because many Christians have unknown faith . That is why it seems like miracles are decreasing in the christendom. They may have joined the Christian faith but couldn't define the faith they accepted to be theirs. Because they did not have time to get the knowledge of those articles they were called to believe on.

every society has their terms and conditions, before you join them you must read and understand the terms and conditions some will ask you to sign it before belonging . No wonder in the Catholic church you need to pass through catechism classes before you become a full member of the church and receive the communion .Although many Catholics today didn't pass through catechism classes in the right sense, rather they will try to fulfill all righteousness. Many will just calm the doctrine just to pass the catechism exam and that is all . Many parishes didn't value the Sunday evening teaching of the doctrine for all the members of church as it was before . All this negligence is the great sin that pushes back the Christian faith. Yet we complain there is no much miracles in the house of God while we didn't have time to know our faith . Whenever you see a member of any church who doesn't know at least 50% of what their community believes, normally stand with one leg at the gate of their community, because every tradition and norm of the church must be so awkward to him.

I met a pastor on a bus one day preaching against other churches, mostly against the Catholic church, when I asked him why, he said that he was a Catholic before until he discovered that Christ was not in the Catholic church then he joined the church he saw Christ in. As we go further in discussion I discovered that he was born in the Catholic church but didn't have a chance to know his faith until another man who have chance for him come into his life and forced him to known little of the Christian faith through his new church. The same as a member of Confraternity of christian doctrine in my Church I have met a lady who come to lean the Christian doctrine (catechism) class after one month of the learning he become more interested at Catholic way of life she complains that her former doesn't have apostolic traditions like Catholic. Do you now see that the problem may not be the Church or religion but lack of the knowledge of the Faith.

Try your Best and known your faith, even if it require you to study your believe like serious university student does, it will help you to increase your faith and miracles in your life.

Story of ignorant airplane cleaner

An Aeroplane cleaner was cleaning the Pilot's cockpit, when he saw a book titled, "*HOW TO FLY AN AIRPLANE FOR BEGINNERS* (Volume 1)
He opened the first (1st) page which said: "To start the engine, press the red button...". He did so, and the airplane engine started... He was happy and opened the next page....:
"To get the airplane moving, press the blue

button... "He did so, and the plane started moving at an amazing speed...
He wanted to fly, so he opened the third (3rd) page which said: To let the airplane fly, please press the green button... "He did so and the plane started to fly...
He was excited...!!
After twenty (20) minutes of flying, he was satisfied, and wanted to land, so he decided to go to the fourth (4th) page... and page four (4) says; "To be able to know how to land a plane, please purchase Volume 2 at the nearest bookshop.

Lesson of conscience
Never attempt anything without complete information
Half Education is not only dangerous but destructive!!! Many Christian are like this ignorant cleaner. We all want to fly with humongous miracles, yet we don't have the knowledge in the faith that will trigger out the fire of our miracles.

Let us meditate a little in the book of mark (10:46-52) Bartimaeus the blind and a beggar heard about Jesus, and know all about what Jesus can do, he said to himself if this man could make a completely dead man to rise again, then he will, (not can) make my eyes to see again he began to study more on what Jesus is doing and where he is going , according to scripture, he asked people beside what is happening around, and he was told that the same Jesus the healer is passing by. This is the poor blind man's efforts to get knowledge and increase his faith.

I believe in the adage that says that knowledge is power . if you also believe with me, stand up and search for the knowledge of your faith, the knowledge will give your faith power to break the chain holding down your spiritual miracles and Holiness.
For your faith determines your success both spiritual and physical.
Believe what you know that you have accepted as faith.

Things you need to know about your faith
(I)What is my faith?
(ii) Is my faith corresponding with that of my community ?
(iii) Is it a true and living faith ?
(iv)What are the powers attached to my faith ?
(v) What are the goals to achieve with this faith
(Vi) Is my faith practicable?

What is my faith

This is when one need to discover what he believed on and what he didn't believe to be his faith

Actually, to identify one's faith is the first step to actuate a strong faith in life .

Good news, God has dealt to every man the measure of faith. Romans 12:3

Nobody can say that "I cannot believe that God can do great miracles in my life or save me, or I cannot believe that God loves me", because we all have a measure of faith. The question is what do you need to do with that measure that God has dealt to you?.

ii) IS MY FAITH CORRESPONDING WITH THAT OF MY COMMUNITY?.

A community is a small or large social unit (a group of living things) that has something in common, such as norms, religion, values, or identity. Communities often share a sense of place that is situated in a given geographical area (e.g. a country, village, town, or neighborhood) or in virtual space through communication platforms.

The English-language word "community" derives from the Old French comuneté, which comes from
the Latin communitas"community", "public

spirit" (from Latin communis, "shared in common").

Human communities may share intent, belief, resources, preferences, needs, and risks in common, affecting the identity of the participants and their degree of cohesiveness.

This comes to say that community as religious have a faith in common .For instance In Christian religion our faith are followings.

THE 15 ARTICLES CHRISTIAN BELIEVED ON

1)we believe in God the Father Almighty,
2) that he is the Creator of Heaven and earth;
3) we believed in Jesus Christ,
4) that He is only Son of our Lord, God
5) that Jesus was conceived by the Holy Spirit
6) that Jesus was born of the Virgin Mary.
7) that Jesus suffered under Pontius Pilate, was crucified, died, and was buried.
8) that Jesus descended to the dead.
9) that Jesus was resurrected On the third day .
10) that Jesus ascended into Heaven

and is seated at the right hand of the God the Father.
11) that He will come again to judge the living and the dead.
12) we believed in the Holy Spirit,
13) in our various Church communities, norms and traditions of the apostles and the communion of Saints,
14) we believed in the forgiveness of sins,
15) we believed in the resurrection of the body, and the life everlasting.

If you called yourself a Christian and your faith is different from the above 15 articles, you should go back and recheck your religion because for me you are not a Christian.

iii) IS IT A TRUE AND LIVING FAITH ?
this is very important to discover for today's Religion, many hangs on the shadows of dead and fallacy faith , doing some sort of negative things, try to cover up their sins in the quote of old testament.

This book has revealed the secret, for you to know which way to follow, remember that if you seek for miracles without faith, you are doomed forever. Miracle doest visit the house of deceivers and that is why some pastors are deceiving themselves and their sheep with magic powers.

Living faith means losing oneself for the sake of God and surrendering one's own pleasure for the pleasure of God. Yes this what Christ teaches in the new testament at math:16v25

For if you want to save your own life, you will lose it; but if you lose your life for my sake, you will find it. This is different from many Christian beliefs today, so my question is, are there Christians?.

I perceive that through believe in Christ fountains of light must accept suffering

To be specific, "suffering" No living faith without suffering

Why me?, Why now?,

What is God doing?. Suffering is a tool God uses to get our attention and to accomplish His purposes in our lives. It is designed to build our trust in the Almighty, but suffering requires the right response if it is to be successful in accomplishing God's purposes. Suffering forces us to turn from trust in our own resources to living by faith in God's resources.

Suffering is not in itself virtuous, nor is it a sign of holiness. It is also not a means of gaining points with God, or of subduing the flesh (as in asceticism). When it is possible, suffering is to be avoided. Christ avoided suffering unless it meant acting in disobedience to the Father's will.

"In the day of prosperity be happy, But in the day of difficulties consider God has made the one as well as the other so that man may not discover anything that will be after him (Eccl. 7:14)

The following questions can help us "consider" in the day of Trauma:
- How should I respond to it?
- How am I corresponding to it?
- Am I learning from it?
- How can God use it in my life?.
- Does my attitude demonstrate faith, love for God and for others, Christ-like

maria Faustina prayer I cherished most .
IN TIMES OF SUFFERING

Oh, if only the suffering soul knew how much God loves it , it would die of joy and excess of happiness some day , we will know the value of suffering , but then we will no longer be able to suffer the present moment is ours (dairy 963)

"My faith, my strength"

O Living Host, support me in this exile, that I may be empowered to walk faithfully in the footsteps of the Savior. I do not ask, Lord, that Thou takest me down from the cross, but I implore Thee to give me the strength to remain steadfast upon it. I want to be stretched out upon the cross as Thou wert, Jesus. I want all the tortures and pains that Thou didst suffer. I want to drink the cup of bitterness to the dregs (dairy 1484).
O my Jesus, give me strength to endure suffering so that I may not make a wry face when I drink the cup of bitterness. Help me Thyself to make my sacrifice pleasing to Thee. May it not be tainted by my self-love. May everything that is in me, both my misery and my strength, give praise to Thee, O Lord (dairy 1740).

C. H. Mackintosh. Said on his article titled (The Living God and a Living Faith.)
I quote, "There is one great substantial fact standing prominently forth on every page of the volume of God, and illustrated in every stage of the history of God's people — a fact of immense weight and moral power at all times, but specially in seasons of darkness, difficulty, and discouragement, occasioned by the low condition of things among those who profess to be on the Lord's side. The fact is this, That faith can

always count on God, and God will always answer faith."

The true purpose of adopting a faith is that one should acquire such certainty concerning God, Who is the fountain head of salvation, as if one can see Him with one's eyes. The wicked spirit of sin seeks to destroy a man and a person cannot escape the fatal poison of sin till he believes with full certainty in the Perfect and Living God and till he knows for certain that God exists, Who punishes the offender and bestows upon a righteous one everlasting joy. It is a common experience that when one believes in the fatal effects of anything one does not have recourse to it. For instance, no one swallows poison consciously. No one deliberately stands in front of a wild tiger. No one deliberately thrusts his hand into the hole of a serpent. Then why does a person commit sin deliberately? The reason is that he has not that certainty in this matter as he has in other matters of the kind that we have mentioned. The first duty of a person, therefore, is to acquire certainty with regard to the existence of God, and to adopt a religion through which this certainty can be acquired so that he should fear God and shun sin. How can such certainty be acquired? It cannot be acquired through mere stories. It cannot be acquired through mere arguments. The only way of acquiring certainty is to experience God repeatedly through converse with Him or through witnessing his extraordinary signs, or by keeping company with someone who has that experience

The purpose of religion is that man should obtain deliverance from his passions and should develop personal love for God Almighty through certain faith in His existence and His perfect attributes. Such love of God is the paradise which will appear in diverse shapes in the hereafter. To be unaware of the true God and to keep away from Him and not to have any love for Him is the hell which will appear in diverse shapes in the hereafter. Thus the true purpose is to have full faith in Him.

iv) WHAT ARE THE GOALS TO ACHIEVE WITH THIS MY FAITH

Every person who wants to be successful sets attainable goals at the start of the year. These goals are in line with our dreams and aspirations, and are meant to guide us regarding what to or what not to do. Have you set your goals for the year?

"Look straight ahead, and fix your eyes on what lies before you. Mark out a straight path for your feet; stay on the safe path. Don't get sidetracked; keep your feet from following evil." – Proverbs 4:25-27

I've heard of fellow believers making or writing down their "faith goals," or goals that they want to achieve by faith in God. Some of these faith goals may include buying a house, acquiring a car, getting promoted on the job, even getting married within the year. While these things are good, why don't we set goals that would both require a higher level of faith and accomplish something that God wants? this one will be added to it as in . But seek ye first the kingdom of God, and his righteousness; and all these things shall be added unto you. Matthew: 6v33

Hebrews 11:1 tells us that "faith is the substance of things hoped for, the evidence of things not seen." We know by faith that there are some things that only God can do.

Three GOALS TO ACHIEVE IN FAITH AS A CHRISTIAN

I charge you to make these things your faith goals every year and trust God

A) Let the Word of God Be Your daily bread

(Psalm 119:97) said, "Oh, how I love your instructions! I think about them all day long." Some might think that it's an easy thing to accomplish, but seriously, many of us even feel sleepy at the thought of reading the Bible. How much more challenging it would be to let it fill our hearts and every thought! Make it your goal to love the Word of God, desiring to have more of it and obeying it daily.

B) Spiritual growth and Not Flesh alone
Walk in the Spirit, and you shall not fulfill the lust of the flesh. For the flesh lusts against the Spirit, and the Spirit against the flesh; and these are contrary to one another, so that you do not do the things that you wish. But if you are led by the Spirit, you are not under the law." (Galatians 5:16-18)
While we're in our earthly bodies, we're sure to face the challenges that normal humans do. However, in Christ we're given both the command to be holy and the power to do it – through the Holy Spirit.
Let's desire to walk in the Spirit and not fulfill the lusts of the flesh this year.

C) Be More Christ-Like Daily
"But those who obey God's Word truly show how completely they love him. That is how we know we are living in him. Those who

say they live in God should live their lives as Jesus did." (1 John 2:5-6)

Christianity's endpoint is the return of Christ to take home His beloved Bride who has journeyed through the process of being made into His likeness. We all know that God wants us to be like Christ (see Romans 8:28-29). Why not desire the same thing? No one will be like Christ the moment we meet Him. Rather, it's through constantly beholding His face that we become like Him. Let's desire to be transformed into His likeness.

"But we all, with unveiled faces, beholding as in a mirror the glory of the Lord, are being transformed into the same image from glory to glory, just as by the Spirit of the Lord." (2 Corinthians 3:18).

v) IS MY FAITH PRACTICABLE?

True Christian faith is not just an abstract, theoretical thing, but something which affects our thoughts, words and actions, and not just on Sundays, but every day of the week see more in chapter four.

"My faith, my strength"

CHAPTER TWO

ARISE AND BELIEVE IN THE ARTICLES.

" very much important"

BELIEVE IN YOUR FAITH

2nd mystery

Miracle of wealth

Jesus told apostle peter to put the fishing net on the right hand side of the river he believed and his net catch multiple of fishes(john:21v6)

He also ask him go to river and put a net the fish you catch open it mouth that he will see a coins, use it and pay for our tax (Matthew 17: 24 - 27) it works because he believed Jesus blindly.

Jesus Feeds 5,000 People with just five loves of bread and 2 fishes (Matthew 14:13-21; Mark 6:30-44; Luke 9:10-17; John 6:1-15)

Let us believe that our wealth will come from God He can bless and multiple our efforts

----

"My faith, my strength"

BELIEVE IN YOUR FAITH

It is chador that many people didn't believe in their faith, still their want Miracle in their life

The worst part of this is that many didn't know their faith . However, he who knows his faith will also know what his faith can work but anyone who doesn't know his faith can't tell exactly what the faith is up to doing . believing in a particular faith is a second step in walk of the five mystery in faith

The Bible teaches us that genuine faith is "more precious than gold that perishes" (1 Peter 1:7). Indeed such faith is going to be "tested by fire". You can expect difficulties and persecutions in your life of faith, as well as blessings. Therefore to encourage you to hold onto and develop your faith, This is when you have to show the world that you really when tribulations and suffering became cumbersome, the life used to be found heavy and difficult to carry or wear. At this time cometh some doubt in one's faith, at a point like this in life I tagged it (cumbersome time in faith).

Let's talk a little about the word cumbersome.

CUMBERSOME

"My faith, my strength"

   This is a heavy or difficult to carry or wear. something undefined . It is so great to define the fear of Christian in this present time. Few Christians have a definite faith due to the heavy difficulties that face Christian lives . The today born new churches believed on what they can benefit from Christ and church only not what did Jesus want from them . which is very contrary to the advice of John s. Kennedy the formal American president, who said think not what America will do for you but what you will do for America . I think this quote I will repeat to all Christian all over the world, (pls think not what Jesus will do for you but first what you will do for Jesus .) although is not the same with john Kennedy meaning because America can not pay your Ransom but Jesus have done that early and ask us to just believe and is well . the bible said at () sick first the kingdom of God and every other thing will be added unto it just like Solomon did at 2 king ().

The conditions of Christian today borders me, this very cumbersome doubt in church beliefs.
Do you notice that corruption is becoming so tantamount while the church keeps increasing Paramountly. This is because we all want it to be sharp, no one ever

remembers the profits of suffering. This is based on the day by day phase that said no one wants to die but they want to go to heaven.

Story of a woman of only child monicy, by name.
survived with only a son after many years of fasting and prayer in marriage . She promised in prayer to give back the son to God if God gave her at least a child , then God contracted with her and gave her a handsome boy , then monicy failed God by over pampering her son. She never for once corrects her son's wrong doing. Instead she will likely say nwadiuko (child is scarce) which makes chiadi to be so proud and rude in character he sold his conscience to the devil which gives him morale to treat neighbors and family members like wide animals . if people complained about him to his mother she would say (hmmm do you know that child is scarce) . monicy forgot all she promised God on the day of her need . The boy keeps growing with extra free hands . One day the people planned to teach him and his mother a lesson because no one has peace of mind about his arrogance. He fell into the plan . you know that an adage said that if a dead dog catches it it will not allow it to know the

"My faith, my strength"

smell of feces. And that a stubborn fowl must hear in a soup pot.

He one day fell into the kidnappers hand. And the question became where to find the guy . she search all over the country with policeman and other caring agents but no way she moved to all the spiritual house she can afford to friends directed her to but no solutions
At this moment , monicy remembered God again as she turned to God and ask for mercy , our merciful God torched the capturers and their released the guy .
What did monicy supposed to do at the second point of answering her play ?. She suppose go to thanksgiving and keep her faith God but instead she continued her way of life and took her son to witch coven for protection and long life .

This is the type of life many Christian live today. Try and believe in your faith we will consider some of the benefits of strong faith.

1)Believing in Faith brings salvation.
(Ephesians 2:8,9). Whosoever believes in Him has eternal life. (John 3:16), and shall not come into judgment, but has passed from death to life. (John 5:24). The just shall

live by faith. (Romans 1:17). having a strong faith is believing in faith

2. Believing in Faith brings answers to prayers. "And whatever things you ask in prayer, really believing, you will receive." (Matthew 21:22). Since God tells us to pray for our daily bread (Matthew 6:11), believing in your faith is therefore a key to our material provision.

3. Believing in Faith brings all the benefits of salvation into our lives (Ephesians 2:8,9). This includes healing, prosperity, peace, love, joy (1 Peter 1:8), deliverance from demons and the curse, sanctification of the mind and emotions (the salvation of the soul) and any other benefit which the word of God promises to us.

4. Believing in Faith is a spiritual force through which our ministry for Christ becomes effective. (Mark 11:23; Matthew 17:19,20). Faith is a major key to ministry success. It brings to you what you need for your ministry, and by imparting it to others through your life and your ministry of God's Word, you enable them to receive the blessings of God's grace mentioned above.

5. In particular, believing in one's faith is the major key for an effective healing and deliverance. Jesus Christ "the same yesterday, today and forever" lives in the Christian (Hebrews 13:8, Galatians 2:20), and through the Christian wants to reveal the power of salvation to men in a way they can see and feel. In this way, our evangelism concerning the Kingdom of God will not be in talk, but in power (1 Corinthians 4:20).

How to Develop a stubborn Faith

We see how important believing in faith is or having a stubborn faith . Yet some people despair here, thinking that they don't have faith. Yet faith comes (Romans 10:17), it can grow and develop. If you are not full of faith today, that doesn't mean you will be that way all your life. You can choose to be a person of strong faith.

Here are ten keys to developing stubborn faith.

1) Gratitude (1 Thessalonians 5:18).

2) Realize that every believer has been given a measure of faith by God (Romans 12:3)
3) Praying in tongues is a key to being full of the Spirit(1 Corinthians 14:4).
4) Listen to the Word of God as much as possible(Romans 10:17)
5) Obey God and the conviction of the Holy Spirit
6) Speak the WORD. By preaching it yourself(Hebrews 3:1)
7) Develop a life of praise and worship. (Hebrews 13:15)
8) Spend as much time as you can with people of the same faith. (Proverbs 13:20).
Proverbs 27:17, "Iron sharpens iron, and one man sharpens the face his neighbor,"
9) Remember that faith works by love (Galatians 5:6).
10) Seek holiness, purity of heart. (Romans 10:10)

Believe in power of Confession and forgiveness

"With the mouth confession is made unto salvation" (Romans 10:10). Since salvation includes many benefits and blessings our right mouth confession is a major key to

receiving what God has provided for us by his grace. Jesus said to his apostles , the sin you forgiven have been forgiven in heaven the one did here on earth is bid forever in heaven.(john :20v27) when you have a completed contrition of your sin and confess it to the priest with the grace of mercy you will automatically be forgiven . but you go about your penance which means trying to pay back the way you go wrong either by attitude , word , work or by prayer also being strongly prepared to avoid the sin and its occasions in the future .
And also confess the word of God

homologeo is a Greek word which means literally "to say the same thing. To confess the Word of God then means to say the same thing as God's Word says. When you say it, it tends to produce faith because in saying it you must also hear it from your own mouth, and hearing the Word causes faith to come (Romans 10:17). In saying the Word yourself, you identify YOURSELF with the truth of God's Word. It is one thing to hear someone else say something, another to say that thing yourself. The more you say God's Word, the more you will believe it, and the more you believe it, the more you will say it.

We should realize that "Death and life is in the power of the tongue, And those who love it will eat its fruit." (Proverbs 18:21). The power of the tongue is in the power of the words we speak. All our words have an effect on the spiritual atmosphere around us, either for good or bad. It is through words that covenants and promises are established. It is through words that our faith or our fears are expressed. Bad words open the door for bad spirits to work. Good words open the door for God and His angels to work.

Angels heed the voice of God's Word (Psalms 103:20). Words are spiritual seeds. Words of life produce life. Words of faith produce faith. Words of love produce love. Words of hope produce hope, and so on. Words of death attract spirits of death, words of doubt attract doubt, words of fear attract spirits of fear, and so on. Therefore we must guard carefully what we SAY. The Bible has much to say on this subject, especially in the Book of Proverbs (e.g. Proverbs 10:19, 20, 31, 32; 12:18, 22; 14:23, 33; 15:1, 4, 28). Jesus said, "But I say to you that for every idle word men may speak, they will give account of it on the day of judgment. For by your words you will be justified, and by your words you will be condemned. " (Matthew 12:36,37). Paul

said, "And WHATEVER you do, IN WORD or deed, do ALL in the name of the Lord Jesus, giving thanks to God the Father through Him." (Colossians 3:17)
A man's belly shall be satisfied with the fruit of his mouth; and with the increase of his lips shall he be filled." (Proverbs 18:20, see Proverbs 12:14). This means that we feed on the words we speak. What we say comes back to affect our own heart and our own spiritual condition. That is another reason why confessing the Word and not negative things will greatly help our faith.

At times it is difficult to speak consistently with what the Bible says because our minds are not sufficiently renewed. We still have doubt in our souls. We must reprogram our subconscious minds to accept God's principles and God's promises without doubt (Romans 12:2). Meditation, repeated pondering, listening to good preaching, confession of the Scripture, as well as informed study will help here. The Word must enter deeply into us. This will change the way we are, the way we speak, the way we respond to difficulties and challenges. If it does not we have been too superficial in our treatment of the Word. We have substituted the mental knowledge and recognition of the words for real meditation and confession.

God talks in faith. God "gives life to the dead and calls those things which do not exist as though they did" (Romans 4:17). Through faith-filled words, God created the universe (Hebrews 11:3). As sons of God we are called to be imitators of God, filled with God's Spirit (Eph 5:1,18). When we are in Christ and we have the promise of God, we have the right to speak about something God has promised as if it existed even before our natural senses are conscious of it. It is our faith that gives substance to this confession of things not seen. For example, if we have believed in God for a car, we can talk about our car before we see it. We should realize that God has already "given us all things that pertain to life and godliness" (2 Peter 1:3) and all spiritual blessings (Ephesians 1:3). But the effective receiving depends on our faith. Faith is confident of the faithfulness of God in His declared promises and talks and acts so, even before the natural eye sees.

as a child / youth we believe in the faith of our parent for that is where we come from until we began to have some doubt on such believe and began to fine it somewhere us . sometimes we get it right sometimes we get it wrong for it is said in Igbo adage that what a man saw while sitting on the ground if a child climb a sycamore tree like zackious he could not see it.

Let's just check if we are making sense with these storylines.

Story of a Thomus fish

A little fish were swimming and discussing with parent fish , perhaps they trying to have some fun along their arena trying to show the little child the boundary do and don't in the river when they saw a piece of meat dangling before them
The younger fish darted toward it with an open mouth. The older father cried out, "Stop"!
"You can't see it, but there is a hook inside that meat. It is connected by an invisible line to a pole outside the water. There is a man holding the pole" and the mother fish said yes is true my child.
the father continue

THE TRUTH is, if you eat the meat, the hook will catch in your jaw and the man will pull you out of the water. He will cut you open with a knife, roast you on a fire and eat you. Then he will throw your remains to his cat."

"My faith, my strength"

The young fish stopped. Then the three swam away. But when the young fish was alone, he thought to himself, "Let me investigate the *truth* for myself and legally verify how accurate these lousy claims are". Armed with those thoughts, he went back to the meat. Immediately, he started investigating by swimming around the meat. He swam above and below it for some time. He swam up and down as far as he could in widening circles around the meat.
After a long search, he said to himself, "I've looked far and wide, and *I haven't found any sign of a man, a pole, a knife, a fire or a cat.* In fact, I've found nothing outside this water we live in" I have come to realize my *truth*"These, " he concluded, must just be stories made up by the old fishes out of jealousy to limit our freedoms in this water. He went back to the meat and ate it. Immediately he ate it, the hook caught in his jaw. He felt himself being yanked out of the water by an outside powerful force. As he fell on the ground outside the water,

He saw a pole, a man and a knife, and a little further, he saw the man's cat sleeping in a shade*.He wished he had believed the its parent fishes words but at that point, his knowledge of *the TRUTH* was useless.

You the reader, isn't this the same story your parents told you about believing the same with them ?. When we tell people to believe in the same faith our old Christian fathers left for us their arguments are," what about those who believe in Allah alone rather than Jesus? What about those who believe in Buddha? How about those who don't believe Jesus but have their own traditional religions? Do you think God can just send people in hell for not believing in Jesus? With arguments, they are doing everything in their power to disapprove the belief that Jesus is the only way to heaven. Some people are swimming around making others believe that there is no heaven or hell..They say the earth was formed by a loud bang I have always asked them ' even if the earth is a product of a loud bang,who caused that bang if not God? To them,they talk of it as an act of matter. To the best of their theoretical knowledge, they swim around looking for miracle centers thinking we are wrong to say " believe in Jesus and develop stubborn faith. They don't know some things are beyond our human mind's comprehension.

The bible does not say Christians will go to heaven through Jesus and Muslims through Allah. It does not name Budha either! It says

Jesus is the only way to heaven. You may not believe it now but a day is coming when reality will sink in you, but it will be too late at that time to reverse the effects of your belief. Atheists should not wait until they're lifted out of the world, only to see God and realize how hell, heaven and see the eternal fire of hell, but unfortunately, of course we will realize when late all along that it was. **THEY FALSE FAITH vs OUR THRU FAITH**, and that will be only when death eventually strikes, but Alas!, It will be "Too late forever"

May God open our eyes to heed to the *TRUTH* while it is useful to us. JESUS said, *"I AM the way, the TRUTH and the life* Nobody goes to the Father without me. Don't swim around the truth like this young fish locking for the miracle of husband, chidi, wealth and money. Believe in the true faith because this the only way to heaven.

CHAPTER THREE

IRREPARABLE

HOPE

AND TRUST

"My faith, my strength"

IRREPARABLE HOPE AND TRUST

3rd MYSTERY

Miracle of calming the storm.

Jesus strengthen His apostles by teaching faith to be fearless
Calming the storm is one of the miracles of Jesus in the Gospels, reported in Matthew 8:23-27, Mark 4:35-41, and Luke 8:22-25. In chapter 14 of Matthew verses 22 -33, After Peter came down out of the ship and walked on the water, he became afraid of the storm and began to sink. He called out to Jesus for help. ... Matthew also notes that the disciples called Jesus the Son of God.
Read more from bible

IRRESISTIBLE HOPE AND TRUST

DEFINITION OF HOPE

Hope is an optimistic state of mind that is based on an expectation of positive outcomes with respect to events and circumstances in one's life or the world at large.
As a verb, its definitions include: "expect with confidence" and "to cherish a desire with anticipation".
Among its opposites
are dejection, hopelessness and despair.

Professor of Psychology Barbara Fredricksonargues, said that hope comes into its own when crisis looms, opening us to new creative possibilities.

The psychologist Charles R. Snyder linked hope to the existence of a goal, combined with a determined plan for reaching that goal:

Alfred Adler had similarly argued for the centrality of goal-seeking in human psychology, as too had philosophical anthropologists like Ernst Bloch.
Snyder also stressed the link between hope and mental willpower, as well as the need for realistic perception of goals.

Hope theory

As a specialist in positive psychology, Snyder studied how hope and forgiveness can impact several aspects of life such as health, work, education, and personal meaning. He postulated that there are three main things that make up hopeful thinking:
Goals – Approaching life in a goal-oriented way.
Pathways – Finding different ways to achieve your goals. Agency – Believing that you can instigate change and achieve these goals.
In other words, hope was defined as the perceived capability to derive pathways to desired goals and motivate oneself via agency thinking to use those pathways.

Snyder argues that individuals who are able to realize these three components and develop a belief in their ability are hopeful people who can establish clear goals, imagine multiple workable pathways toward those goals, and persevere, even when obstacles get in their way.

Snyder proposed a "Hope Scale" which considered that a person's determination to achieve their goal is their measured hope. Snyder differentiates between adult-measured hope and child-measured hope. The Adult Hope Scale by Snyder contains 12 questions; 4 measuring 'pathways thinking', 4 measuring 'agency thinking', and 4 that are simply fillers. Each subject responds to each question using an 8-point scale. Fibel and Hale measure hope by combining Snyder's Hope Scale with their own Generalized Expectancy for Success Scale (GESS) to empirically measure hope. Snyder regarded that psychotherapy can help focus attention on one's goals, drawing on tacit knowledge of how to reach them. Similarly, there is an outlook and a grasp of reality to hope, distinguishing No Hope, Lost Hope, False Hope and Real Hope, which differ in terms of viewpoint and realism.

IRRESISTIBLE Hope in faith irresistible

Hope is a key concept in most major world religions, often signifying the "hoper" believes an individual or a collective group will reach a concept of heaven. Depending on the religion, fearless hope can be seen as a prerequisite for and/or byproduct of spiritual attainment. Hope is one of the three theological virtues of the Christian religion, alongside faith and love.

Hope" in the Holy Bible means "a strong and confident expectation" of future reward (Titus 1:2). In modern terms,fearless hope is akin to trust and a confident expectation" Apostle paul argued that hope was a source of salvation for Christians: "For in hope we have been saved...if we hope for what we do not see, with perseverance we wait eagerly for it" (Romans 8:25).
According to the Holman Bible Dictionary, hope is a "[t]rustful expectation...the anticipation of a favorable outcome under God's guidance." In The Pilgrim's Progress in earth, it is fearless Hope who comforts Christian in cumbersome Doubting Castle. No fear of hoping with faith.

Irresistible Hope as a therapy

Irresistible Hope has the ability to help people heal faster and easier. Individuals who maintain fearless hope, especially when battling with serious illness, significantly enhance their chances of recovery. This is important because numerous people with chronic, physical, or mental illness believe that their condition is stable and that they have little chance of recovery. If health care providers begin to recognize the importance of hope in the recovery process, then they can learn to instill hope within their patients; this would enable patients to develop healthy coping strategies and therefore improve their physical and emotional well being. Shaping people's beliefs and expectations to be more hopeful and optimistic is an essential component of positive psychology. In general, people who possess fearless hope and think optimistically have a greater sense of well being in addition to the improved health outcomes outlined above.
Bible cont remember
Positive psychologists teach strategies to help boost people's hope and optimism, which would benefit individuals coping with

illness by improving their life satisfaction and recovery process.

The inclusion of hope in treatment programs has potential in both physical and mental health settings. Hope as a mechanism for improved treatment has been studied in the contexts of PTSD, chronic physical illness, and terminal illness, among other disorders and ailments.
 Within mental health practice, clinicians have suggested using hope interventions as a supplement to more traditional cognitive behavioral therapies. In terms of support for physical illness, research suggests that hope can encourage the release of endorphins and enkephalins, which help to block pain.

Great men's quote on irresistible hope.

Hopeful, we are halfway to where we want to go; hopeless, we are lost forever. (Lao Tzu)
Keep a little fire burning; however small, however hidden. (Cormac McCarthy)

Two words will help you cope when you run low on hope: accept and trust. (Charles R. Swindoll)
Courage is like love; it must have hope for nourishment. (Napoleon Bonaparte)

I knew life began where I stood in the dark, looking out into the light. (Yusef Komunyakaa)

Patience and fortitude conquer all things. (Ralph Waldo Emerson)

Not to give up under any circumstances should be the motto of our life: we shall try again and again, and we are bound to succeed. There will be obstacles, but we have to defy them. The goal is ahead of you. If you do not give up, you are bound to reach your destined goal. (Sri Chinmoy)

No matter where you are on your journey, that's exactly where you need to be. The next road is always ahead. (Oprah Winfrey)

irresistible hope is a target to success (magnus I Nnaji)

When you get into a tight place and everything goes against you, till it seems as though you could not hang on a minute longer, never give up then, for that is just the place and time that the tide will turn. (Harriet Beecher Stowe)

Fearless in prospecting is a target to success (magnus I Nnaji)

Restart from failure is a powerful fearless hope (magnus I Nnaji)

All human wisdom is summed up in two words; wait and hope. (Alexandre Dumas)

Irresistible Trust

Trouble and tribulation are a little tougher because there is usually less to say, and nothing much you can do when people are extremely ill or have just lost a loved one. Thankfully God knew that we would experience both good and bad in life and He has provided words to help us celebrate as well as mourn during those times.
In Psalm 27 David provides an example of the kind of attitude a believer should have when facing tough moments. This attitude can be summarized in a phrase - irreparable trust.

In this canticle, David however, describes the many fearless trust that a true child of God should have because of his relationship with God.
Fearless trust
Some people have the wrong idea of trust. They think trust is:
Crossing their fingers and hoping for the best.A type of resignation, "Oh well we have no choice, might as well pray."Blind faith and optimism "It will all work out okay."
David shows in his prayer that fearless trust in God has much more noble and specific qualities than these.

1) irresistible Trust is unshakable

1 The Lord is my light and my salvation—
whom shall I fear?
The Lord is the stronghold of my life—
of whom shall I be afraid?
2When the wicked advance against me
to devour me,
it is my enemies and my foes
who will stumble and fall.
3 Though an army besiege me,
my heart will not fear;
though war break out against me,
Even then I will be confident.

In this first few verses, David gives reasons why he must be fearless in trusting in the Lord. The Lord is the one who enlightens him, gives him understanding. The Lord is the one who will ultimately save his soul. David compares the damage that his enemies can do to him against the ultimate power of the Lord and concludes that there is nothing to be afraid of. Of course his point is that God has given him the ability to understand that his enemies can only harm him physically - and then only some of the time.

His soul, however, is safe with God; it is out of the reach of his enemies so he has fearless trust in God.

2. Irresistible Trust is Joyful,
4. One thing I ask from the Lord, this only do I seek: that I may dwell in the house of the Lord all the days of my life,to gaze on the beauty of the Lord and to seek him in his temple.
5 For in the day of trouble he will keep me safe in his dwelling;he will hide me in the shelter of his sacred tent
and set me high upon a rock.
6 Then my head will be exalted above the enemies who surround me; at his sacred tent I will sacrifice with shouts of joy; I will sing and make music to the Lord.

David speaks with confident anticipation of the final victory that he will eventually have, and it leads him to praise God who will provide it. He says that through his trouble he has remained close to God by worshiping Him and meditating on His word. This experience has focused his attention away from his problems and onto the Lord. The result is a grateful and joyful spirit of praise.
In times of trouble and tragedy the first thing we want to do is go into a corner and hide -

retreat from the world and from the Lord as well (or complain, blame and criticize). David does the opposite.

3. Irresistible Trust is Confident
7 Hear my voice when I call, Lord; be merciful to me and answer me.
8 My heart says of you, "Seek his face!" Your face, Lord, I will seek.
9 Do not hide your face from me, do not turn your servant away in anger;
you have been my helper. Do not reject me or forsake me, God my Savior.
10 Though my father and mother forsake me, the Lord will receive me.
David reviews his past experiences with the Lord and notes that God has always answered, always helped, always saved him in one way or another. He says that his parents have left him (probably because they died) but God will never leave him.

David demonstrates that if our trust is in the Lord it is surer than even the trust we have in our parents who are loyal and loving but weak and temporal.

Final Encouragement

11 Teach me your way, Lord; lead me in a straight path
because of my oppressors.
12 Do not turn me over to the desire of my foes, for false witnesses rise up against me, spouting malicious accusations.
13 I remain confident of this: I will see the goodness of the Lord in the land of the living.
14 Wait for the Lord; be strong and take heart
and wait for the Lord. Once he has described the kind of trust that he has in the Lord and why:
Having encouraged his readers to trust God David leaves them with a final exhortation about what to do when in times of trouble.

in addition to trusting the Lord.
VS. 11-12 - First he asks God for two things.
1. Enlightenment - vs. 11
2. Protection - vs. 12

In vs.23 David says that unless he had trusted the Lord the way he did and prayed the way he did - he would have fallen into despair.1. Be Patient
2. Be Strong and Courageous.

Great men's quotes on irresistible Trust

I'm not upset that you lied to me, I'm upset that from now on I can't believe you.
(Friedrich Nietzsche)

All the world is made of faith, trust, and pixie dust.
(J.M. Barrie, Peter Pan)

I don't trust people who don't love themselves and tell me, 'I love you.' ...
There is an African saying which is: Be careful when a naked person offers you a shirt.
(Maya Angelou)

Trust no man for human heart is deceiving rather have an irresistible trust in faith with God
(Magnus I Nnaji)

The best way to find out if you can trust somebody is to trust them.
(Ernest Hemingway)

Have enough courage to trust love one more time and always one more time.
(William Shakespeare,

All's Well That Ends Well)

All the world is made of faith, trust, and pixie dust.
(J.M. Barrie, Peter Pan)

I don't trust people who don't love themselves and tell me, 'I love you.' ...
There is an African saying which is: Be careful when a naked person offers you a shirt.
(Maya Angelou)

The best way to find out if you can trust somebody is to trust them.
(Ernest Hemingway)

I don't trust anybody. Not anybody. And the more that I care about someone, the more sure I am they're going to get tired of me and take off.
(Rainbow Rowell, Fangirl)

"My faith, my strength"

This book would only exist in my dreams without you, my rock and guiding light. Your presence and support have been invaluable to me and I am forever grateful for your unwavering presence in my life.

CHAPTER FOUR

TAKE A POSITIVE ACTIONS

TAKE A POSITIVE ACTIONS

4th Mystery

The Miracle Of Healing

Jesus healed a lot of patients all because they have their faith and believe without doubt .And real action to attract their healing miracles.mark 5;22:43

....

faith into action is not as difficult as it may seem. Hebrews chapter 11 verses 1 - 3 and 12 verses 1 - 3
True faith is practical faith, with examples Everyone, even the most committed Atheist, has faith of some kind,
and that faith always has some practical outworking.
Theoretical faith is OK up to a point
but is not much good if it has no everyday use or application.
For example, when we board a bus or plane

"My faith, my strength"

We have faith that the driver or pilot is fit and well trained.
If we did not, we just wouldn't travel.
For example, when we sit on a chair,
We have faith that it will bear our weight and not collapse under us.

If we did not have that faith, we would remain standing.
For example, when we buy something in a shop,
we have faith that it will do whatever we expect it to do, or we would not buy it.
And we must have faith, trust, confidence in our friends
and hopefully in each other gathered here, or we would live very solitary, lonely lives.
James 2:14-26
along with his works, and faith was brought to Faith without Works Is Dead

14 What good is it, my brothers and sisters,[a]if you say you have faith but do not have works? Can faith save you? 15 If a brother or sister is naked and lacks daily food, 16 and one of you says to them, "Go in peace; keep warm and eat your fill," and yet you do not supply their bodily needs, what is the good of that? 17 So faith by itself, if it has no works, is dead.

18 But someone will say, "You have faith and I have works." Show me your faith apart from your works, and I by my works will show you my faith. 19 You believe that God is one; you do well. Even the demons believe—and shudder. 20 Do you want to be shown, you senseless person, that faith apart from works is barren? 21 Was not our ancestor Abraham justified by works when he offered his son Isaac on the altar? 22 You see that faith was active completion by the works. 23 Thus the scripture was fulfilled that says, "Abraham believed God, and it was reckoned to him as righteousness," and he was called the friend of God. 24 You see that a person is justified by works and not by faith alone. 25 Likewise, was not Rahab the prostitute also justified by works when she welcomed the messengers and sent them out by another road? 26 For just as the body without the spirit is dead, so faith without works is also dead.

Acts 9:36-42
36 In Joppa there was a disciple named Tabitha (in Greek her name is Dorcas); she was always doing good and helping the poor. 37 About that time she became sick and died, and her body was washed and placed in an upstairs room. 38 Lydda was

"My faith, my strength"

near Joppa; so when the disciples heard that Peter was in Lydda, they sent two men to him and urged him, "Please come at once!"
39 Peter went with them, and when he arrived he was taken upstairs to the room. All the widows stood around him, crying and showing him the robes and other clothing that Dorcas had made while she was still with them.
40 Peter sent them all out of the room; then he got down on his knees and prayed. Turning toward the dead woman, he said, "Tabitha, get up." She opened her eyes, and seeing Peter she sat up. 41 He took her by the hand and helped her to her feet. Then he called for the believers, especially the widows, and presented her to them alive. 42 This became known all over Joppa, and many people believed in the Lord.

There is nothing in the world more practical than faith. It may seem to the naturalist a very dreamy, speculative thing, but when we stop to think, we shall readily see that the most practical thing in life is confidence. Like the law of gravitation which holds the universe together, the principle of cohesion that binds human society is confidence between man and man. Take it away from the home and where would the family be? Take it away from business and where would your bank and stock exchanges be? Take it away from the State and we have revolution, anarchy, socialism and the uprooting of the foundations of society.

A practical Christian faith must be holy According to the voice of the bishop at the 1979 Lenten pastoral gathering . which he themed. "you too are called to holiness " many Christians today think that holy life is main for the clergy only . but the truth is that all Christians are called to holiness . for I am the lord your God be holy for I am holy (Lev. 11 : 44) in practice what is to be holy? This is well expressed in the God ten commandments. Of which Jesus summarized to be The Great Commandment (or Greatest Commandment) is a name used in the New Testament to describe the first of two commandments cited by Jesus in Matthew 22:35–40 and Mark 12:28–34. These two commandments are paraphrases taken from the Old Testament and are commonly seen as important practice to all the Christians In Mark, when asked "which is the great commandment in the law?", the Greek New Testament reports that

Jesus answered, "Hear, O Israel! The Lord our God, The Lord is One; Thou shalt love the Lord thy God with all thy heart, and with all thy soul, and with all thy mind" before also referring to a second commandment, "Thou shalt love thy neighbor as thyself." Most Christian denominations consider these two commandments to be the core of correct Christian faith and practice.
A practical Christian faith. Must be (tabahums)
1) tolerance,
2)Angelic understanding,
3 blind obedience
4) Ardent charity
5) Heroic Patience
6) unconditional forgiveness
7) mental Prayerful
8)Surpassing purity

Which call to fourteen humanitarian actions that solve human problems. man need to give back to the world

Fourteen Humanitarian Actions

1 Less human hunger,
2 quench human thirsty,

3 Cover human naked,
4 Shelter human,
5 Heal human sickness,
6 Accord rightful judgment to human
7 Bury the dead.
8 Instruct the ignorant ones.
9 Counsel the doubtful.
10 Admonish the errors.
11 Bear patiently those who wrong us.
12 Forgive offenses.
13 comfort the afflicted.
14 Praying for everyone.

In Matthew 25:40 And the King shall answer and say unto them, Verily I say unto you, Inasmuch as ye have done it unto one of the least of these my brethren, ye have done it unto me

We are all called to be holy, to live lives of grace, but how do we put our faith in Jesus Christ into action on a daily basis?

Here are some actions that may help you get started:
1. Receive the Sacraments or any way your church calls their members to holy life Attend Mass / services and go to confession/counseling. These acts not only

bring grace, but tend to lighten any burdens you may be carrying.

2. Limit your TV time. Don't watch TV that portrays your faith relationship

3. Pray for everyone at your reach , even someone who has wronged you. And forgive them willingly. It doesn't really matter if they are sorry for what they did to you or if they even know they hurt you. (Very difficult task) but you have started developing a strong power in spiritual reign if you can fight to get this grace . yes it is a (great grace).

4. Don't gossip, always stand up for someone.

6. Read good books like Bible and other spiritual books,   social and motivation selections that will bring you back to human reasoning.

7. Stop complaining and start thanking God for your blessings.

8. Hold your tongue. A big part of being patient is just shutting up.

9. Organize your house and your mind.

10. Pray without ceasing. Paul wrote in 1 Thessalonians, "Rejoice always. Pray without ceasing. In all circumstances give thanks, for this is the will of God for you in Christ Jesus."As you may have heard before, prayer four general parts: Adoration – Praising God Contrition – Confessing your sins Thanksgiving. Asking for things Adoration is the first because it's the most important. God is our creator, our savior, our healer, our everything and He deserves to be praised all the time. So don't just pray, adore Him, and do some work of faith which is full of suffering. Yes .Get ready to carry your cross (suffering) For it is a way of human purification.

Let us recap with this short story.

How smithman refines a silver

A group of prayer team were in a cenacle on the discussion stage, one opened the book of Malachi chapter three(3)As they were studying, they came across verse three, which says: "He will sit as a refiner and purifier of silver." This verse puzzled them and they wondered what this statement meant about the character and nature of God. One of them offered to find out the process of refining silver and get back to the group at their next cenacle day. That week, this young lady called up a silversmith and made an appointment to watch him at work. She didn't mention anything about the reason for her interest beyond her curiosity about the process of refining silver.

As she watched the silversmith, he held a piece of silver over the fire and let it heat up. He explained that in refining silver, one needed to hold the silver in the middle of the fire where the flames were hottest so as to burn away all the impurities. The woman thought about God holding us in such a hot spot then she thought again about the verse, that "He sits as a refiner and purifier of silver." She asked the silversmith if it was true that he had to sit there in front of the fire the whole time the silver was being refined. The man answered saying, he not only had to sit there holding the silver, but he had to keep his eyes on the silver the entire time it was in the fire. If the silver was left a moment too long in the flames, it would be destroyed.

The young lady was silent for a moment. Then she asked the silversmith, "How do you know when the silver is fully refined?" He smiled at her and answered, "Oh, that's easy - when I see my image in it.".If today you are feeling the heat of the fire, remember that God has His eye on you and will keep watching you until He sees His image in you. that is at your point of total purification.

Let this be a learning instrument to all of us.

CHAPTER FIVE

HOLD ON

PERSISTENCE

5th MYSTERY HOLD ON PERSISTENCE

The Parable of the Persistent Widow
Luke 18:1-8

1, Then He spoke a parable to them, that men always ought to pray and not lose heart, 2 saying: "There was in a certain city a judge who did not fear God nor [a]regard man. 3 Now there was a widow in that city; and she came to him, saying, [b]'Get justice for me from my adversary.' 4 And he would not for a while; but afterward he said within himself, 'Though I do not fear God nor regard man, 5 yet because this widow troubles me I will [c]avenge her, lest by her continual coming she weary me.' "

6 Then the Lord said, "Hear what the unjust judge said. 7 And shall God not avenge His own elect who cry out day and night to Him, though He bears long with them? 8 I tell you that He will avenge them speedily.

Persistence

simple mean, the fact of continuing in an opinion or course of action in spite of difficulty or opposition.

In Luke 18:1-8 above.
Jesus tells a story to help the listeners understand the need for persistence in prayer. There are details in this story that could easily slip by those of us living in the western culture of the 21st century. For those listening as Jesus spoke, the details of this story would pique their interest.

Widows had no voice in the culture of the 1st century. A widow would never experience "her day in court," in the formal court setting. This widow was pestering the judge on his time. Perhaps it was as the judge walked to and from work. Maybe she called out her injustice for all in the street to hear. Regardless of how she accomplished it, she was relentless. Her desperate need drove her to repeatedly petition.

Jesus uses different words than I would to describe the judge. I would say something like; there was a judge who was a huge jerk. Lest you think the widow represents you and me and the judge represents God, I'll refer you back to a previous, similar story of Jesus in Luke 11. God is good. He is just. He longs to meet the needs of His children.

The Importance of Persistence in Prayer

Before telling this story, Jesus tells His listeners it only takes a small amount of faith, He tells them perilous, unjust, and terrible times will come. Then Jesus tells them the importance of consistent and persistent prayer.

It is easy to have the injustice, suffering, and evil in the world drive you to your knees in prayer. It's more difficult to continue to pray when it seems like there is no answer. Jesus' conclusion takes the form of a question—are you willing to continue to pray when your timeline and God's timeline aren't in synchronization?

Jesus is telling His followers to continue to pray when circumstances don't make sense. Jesus is telling His followers to be like the widow, one without station, one without rights to request relief or justice, one without means to change her situation but one who would not stop asking. Jesus was telling His followers to have the faith it takes to keep asking when there is no immediate answer. Trust to the end, when the Son of Man comes pray through the dark night replace despair with faith that God will make injustice into justice and sorrow into joy.

Perseverance is vital to growing in your faith, and God wants his people to persevere no matter what happens, so we have to learn how to overcome obstacles, difficulties, trials, and tribulation to experience victory in Christ.

My story of Persistence

Rita and I went through the drive . Rita got plantain chips, since I was driving and not hungry, I got nothing. I wasn't hungry until I saw Rita's plantain chips. I asked her for one chip. She ignored me. I asked again and her reply was a glib, "Why didn't you order something?" I quickly spilled out all the reasons I didn't order. I'm sure I sounded like an auctioneer. I knew I needed to make my plea quickly because Rita didn't stop eating during my diatribe. My final plea was, "I don't know why you can't give me one chip!"

Rita stopped eating, looked at me and quietly said, "If I give you a chip, will you shut up?". "YES!!!", I exclaimed. We both burst out in uproarious laughter. Rita is my baby sister.!

I truly enjoyed my plantain chips. Persistence pays!

Relationship between Failure and persistence.

Failure and persistence go hand in glove, don't they? But not everyone can muster the success of these story examples of failure and persistence. We can all learn a ton from these examples and personalities. And when applied, these lessons can be the difference.

Story Examples of Fail and persist heroes

Tom Watson

Failure can often be the highway to success. Tom Watson Sr. (of IBM fame)

"My faith, my strength"

said, "If you want to succeed, double your failure rate." If you study history, you will find that all stories of success are also stories of great failures. But people don't see the failures. They only see one side of the picture and they say that person had lots of luck on his side: "He must have been at the right place at the right time."

I spent the first 17 years of my career at IBM before they sold the division I worked in. I learned a great deal about Tom Watson in those years. He was an awesome example of persistence in both business and life.

Abraham Lincoln

There is probably no better example of failure and persistence that I know of. Let me share Lincoln's life history with you. This was a man who failed in business at the age of 21 ; was defeated in a legislative race at age 22; failed again in business at age 24; overcame the death of his sweetheart at age 26; had a nervous breakdown at age 27; lost a congressional race at age 34; lost a senatorial race at age 45; failed in an effort to become vice-president at age 47; lost a senatorial race at age 49; and was elected president of the United States at age 52.

Would you dare call him a failure? He could have quit anywhere along the line. But to Lincoln, defeat was a detour and not a dead end. And a great source of learning.

Colonel Sanders
Colonel Sanders at age 65, with a beat-up car and a $100 check from Social Security, realized he had to do something. He remembered his mother's recipe and went out selling. How many doors did he have to knock on before he got his first order? It is estimated that he had knocked on more than a thousand doors before he got his first order.How many of us quit after three tries, ten tries, a hundred tries, and then we say we tried as hard as we could? Quite a lesson of persistence for us all, isn't it?.

Wright Brothers
A New York Times editorial on December 10, 1903, questioned the wisdom of the Wright Brothers who were trying to invent a machine, heavier than air that would fly. One week later, at Kitty Hawk, the Wright Brothers took their famous flight.

Walt Disney

As a young cartoonist, Walt Disney faced many rejections from newspaper editors, who said he had no talent. Even fired from one who told him he lacked imagination and original ideas.

One day a minister at a church hired him to draw some cartoons. Disney was working out of a small mouse infested shed near the church. After seeing a small mouse, he was inspired. That was the start of Mickey Mouse.

How many people would have received the spark of inspiration from that source? Not many I'm afraid.

W. Clement Stone

Have you ever heard of W. Clement Stone, the fantastic self-builder model? He was just 3 when his father died, leaving nothing but gambling debts and his wife and son in poverty. At age 6, he was selling newspapers on the street to help support his family.

He frequently told the story of his early business life which started with the selling of newspapers in restaurants. At the time, this was a very novel thing to do, which deviated dramatically from the normal practice of young boys hawking newspapers on street corners.

This story showed the persistence, style and initiative of Stone ... one that would stay with him for his entire very successful career.

Thomas Edison
One day a partially deaf four year old kid came home with a note in his pocket from his teacher, "Your Tummy is too stupid to learn, get him out of the school." His mother read the note and answered, "My Tommy is not stupid to learn, I will teach him myself."

And that Tommy grew up to be the great Thomas Edison. Thomas Edison had only three months of formal schooling and he was partially deaf.

Key Takeaways
Do you consider any of these people failures? They succeeded in spite of problems, not in the absence of them. But to the outside world, it appears as though they just got lucky.

Successful people don't do great things, they only do small things in a great way.

"My faith, my strength"

All success stories are stories of great failures. The only difference is that every time they failed, they bounced back. This is called failing forward, rather than backward. You learn and move forward. Learn from your failure and keep up your persistence.

All you get is what you
bring to the fight. And that fight gets better every day you learn and apply new ideas.

When things are not what you want them to be, what's most important is your next steps.

Never Give Up Your Dream, Be faithful.

All of the mentioned heroes I guest hold on their faith why passing through their lines of success .why not stand still and persevere till your success rip both physical and spiritual. It will just cost time and pain only.

Benefits of Persistence

"A lizard can be caught with the hand, yet it is found in palaces of the great kings."

What is the lesson from this little creature? It teaches the rewards of persistence which "takes it to the top."

"My faith, my strength"

A great philosopher said, "The race is not always to the swift but to those who keep on running." Among other things, fulfilling God's will for our lives means reaching our total God given human and spiritual potential. We don't have to be geniuses to do this, but we do need to be persistent and keep on regardless of our circumstances.

Saint Paul encountered all sorts of trials and persecutions. He was stoned, whipped and shipwrecked, beaten, and thrown into prison and left for dead for promoting Christdom. He accepted firsthand what it was to experience hunger, loneliness, and cold. The interesting thing about this is that he penned some of his great letters to the churches while in prison.

God has a plan and life purpose for each of us, to achieve it, it won't happen without these four key points: dedication, commitment, hard work, and persistence. As Paul said, "It is God himself in his mercy, who has given us this wonderful work … and so we never give up.

"My faith, my strength"

Some biblical Quotes for persistence

Galatians 6:9 And let us not grow weary of doing good, for in due season we will reap, if we do not give up.

Luke 11:9-10   Proverbs 24:16
Luke 11:5-10   Hebrews 12:1-2
James 1:1-27   1 Corinthians 15:58
Revelation 2:10   2 Kings 2:1-15

1 Thessalonians 5:17 Pray without ceasing,11)
James 1:12; Blessed is the man who remains steadfast under trial, for when he has stood the test he will receive the crown of life, which God has promised to those who love him.

Proverbs 12:27   2 Corinthians 4:8-9
Romans 2:7   1 Thessalonians 5:21
Matthew 15:22-28   Genesis 32:24-28

Hebrews 13:15;Through him then let us continually offer up a sacrifice of praise to God, that is, the fruit of lips that acknowledge his name.

James 1:2 Titus 2:2
Ephesians 6:18 Genesis 18:23-33 24)
Galatians 2:1-21 Colossians 4:2

1 Chronicles 16:11; Seek the Lord and his strength; seek his presence continually!

James 5:11 2 Timothy 2:12
2 Thessalonians 3:5 Romans 12:12
Romans 5:3-5 Luke 13:6-9
Mark 10:46-51 Hebrews 10:36

Romans 5:4 And endurance produces character, and character produces hope,

Matthew 24:13 Matthew 15:21-28
Revelation 3:11 Revelation 3:10
Revelation 2:19 Revelation 2:2-3
1 Timothy 6:12 43) 1 Timothy 4:16
Romans 5:3 John 20:24
1 John 2:19 2 Peter 1:6
2 Peter 1:1-21 James 1:4

James 1:3 For you know that the testing of your faith produces steadfastness.

2 Thessalonians 1:4 1 Corinthians 16:13
Acts 14:22 Luke 21:19
Matthew 10:22 Job 17:9
2 Chronicles 15:7 Revelation 14:12
2 Peter 1:5-7 1 Peter 5:8
1 Peter 4:12.

www.ingramcontent.com/pod-product-compliance
Lightning Source LLC
Chambersburg PA
CBHW030445220526
45464CB00006B/2426